WALK IN PEACE

Legends and Stories of the Michigan Indians

by Simon Otto

Illustrations by
Kayle Crampton

Michigan Indian Press
Grand Rapids Inter-Tribal Council

The publication of this book has been made possible by a grant from the Administration for Native Americans.

Edited by M. T. Bussey

Published by The Michigan Indian Press
Grand Rapids Inter-Tribal Council
45 Lexington N.W.
Grand Rapids, Michigan 49504

Copyright © 1990
ISBN 0-9617707-5-9

Cover illustration by Kayle Crampton
Cover design by Lynne Gort
Printed by West Michigan Printing, Inc.
840 Ottawa Ave., N.W., Grand Rapids, Michigan

Preface

These legends and stories have come from my own memories. They were originally told by Indian elders, my grandfather, father, mother, medicine men, a medicine woman and various others with whom I came in contact in my early life and in later years. The closeness of the earth in the sense of being part of Mother Earth has prompted me to share my thoughts with one and all.

Some of these writings may seem strange, but from the world and mind of the Indian, they are all real. They are part of our life, heritage, and culture.

Anyone who does not agree fully to the language and the material in these writings must realize that all tribes, bands, and villages have their own unique versions of Indian lore, even though these villages might have only been a few miles apart. This author respects all varying versions of the same basic legend themes and does not intend that only his stories be rigidly authentic. Legends grow from different circumstances and are told in highly personal styles. There are many varied tribal dialects in the Indian language. Moreover, the legends and stories differ in detail but concur, generally. That the legend itself can enhance the teaching of Native American culture, is of the greater importance.

Simon Otto

Editor's note — The word Anishnabe (singular), Anishnabek (plural) found in these writings, is an Odawa/Ojibwe word meaning the first or original people. It is the word we use to identify ourselves. The name Nanaboozhoo, which also appears in the text, is the name of the hero and prankster with magical powers from Anishnabe legends.

Dedication

I dedicate these thoughts in writing to my wife,
Mary, who inspired me to put these legends and stories
on paper to share.

Table of Contents

Dog Legend

In the early days when Mother Earth was yet growing, all the animals could talk and understand one another. Each kind of animal had already selected a site where they wanted to live. Muk-aw-gee (Dog) and his mate chose a site far from the village of the Anishnabek, for they were not yet real friends, only acquaintances.

Mukawgee would pass the village on his daily walks. He wandered past the hillside where Nanaboozhoo had his favorite resting spot. Nanaboozhoo often greeted him and he noticed that Mukawgee always seemed happy and care-free. One day Nanaboozhoo invited him up for a cold drink of water and to rest a little. From that day on, Mukawgee stopped regularly to pass the time of day. Soon the two became fast friends.

As the years passed, Mukawgee's children grew up and left home. As they wandered and settled with their mates, they produced different breeds of many sizes and colors. Soon, Mother Earth had quite an assortment of dogs.

Then one day Mukawgee's mate went on the long walk. Now he was all alone. He had no one to talk to and his home was so empty. His mate was gone and his children were scattered all over Mother Earth.

On his daily walk he passed his friend's hillside home and stopped to talk with Nanaboozhoo. He told him of his loneliness and that he had no enjoyment in life anymore. Mukawgee's happy, contented look was gone.

Nanaboozhoo felt sorry for his old friend. How could he help him to be his old self again? He asked Mukawgee if he wanted to stay with him for awhile. Mukawgee pondered this and decided that it would be better to live with someone and not be alone. Soon they shared the same wigwam.

Many days passed into years. Nanaboozhoo and Mukawgee were inseparable and very happy. Thus the friendship between dog and man began, so long ago when Mother Earth was young.

The Legend of the Pike

When the Great Spirit created Mother Earth and all forms of life, he placed in each and every one certain attributes that would identify them and yet set them apart. For instance, the snowshoe rabbit changes colors for protection and the weasel turns white in the wintertime. Birds migrate and some animals sleep through the winter in hibernation.

The Anishnabek have their own explanations for the ways of nature. These stories have been passed on, from generation to generation, to teach about all of the creatures that live on the Earth Mother. One such story is the pike legend.

At one time, Ke-no-zhay (Pike) had a short, fat head and a thin body. One day he was terribly hungry and looking for a meal. As he swam through the weeds, he searched for the tastier minnows. This day, the minnows were not hiding in the weeds. They decided to feed along the wooded shoreline, where the bugs and larvae were more abundant.

The little minnows were up in a shallow cove, sheltered on each side by tall cedar trees. Many cedars from previous years of storms had blown over and were lying submerged on the lake bottom. Many water insects and larvae lived in and around these logs.

As the small minnows darted in and out, feeding, they didn't know that Kenozhay was slowly approaching in the shallow water. Kenozhay thought to himself, "Now I have them trapped up here in the shallow water. They have no weeds to hide in, just those old logs. I can get around those easily enough." As he turned, he saw one particular minnow that would be good for a meal. Just then, three or four more approached. This made Kenozhay excited and even hungrier. He looked and tried to decide which one to go after. Now, one minnow was always alert for predators. As this guard was looking, she saw Kenozhay, skulking in the shadows of the logs. She told the other minnows and they made a quick plan. They usually swam in a bunch, but this time, they decided to split up and hide behind the logs where Kenozhay couldn't get to them.

Now, Kenozhay was familiar with the minnow's pattern of swimming off in a bunch. He knew that all he had to do was to swim into them and he would get at least one. Then they would regroup and the same process would follow again. Little did he know that the minnows had changed their plan.

He lay in wait until the time was right. He quickly swam towards the minnows, expecting them to swim off. Instead, they caught him off guard. Frustrated, he kept swimming around, but the minnows were well hidden in the logs. Kenozhay couldn't get near them, so he decided to hide and try again. He tried and tried, but still no minnows. Now he was angry and said, "I'll get them yet." He saw a minnow in a hole and thought that he could squeeze in and get it. He tried, but his nose was too big. He kept trying and each time he would get a little farther. This kept up and finally he was able to get into the log, but the minnow had already gone out another hole. Suddenly it was easier, because his nose had become long and flat.

All of which goes to show that perseverance and frustration doesn't always guarantee success, but may instead get your nose out of joint.

Turtle Gets A Shell

It was one of those days when Nanaboozhoo was in a strange mood. He had just awakened from a deep sleep that was disturbed by the noisy quarreling and scolding of the bluejays. He was a bit cranky; his sleep was disturbed and besides that, he was hungry. His first thought was to go down to the village and find something to eat.

Entering the village, he came across some men cooking fish. They had their camp located close to the water and Nanaboozhoo spied many fish cooking over a fire. Now, being very hungry, he asked for something to eat. The men were happy to give him some, but cautioned him that it was hot. Not heeding their warning, he quickly grabbed the fish and burned his hand. He ran to the lake to cool it off in the water. Still unsteady from his deep sleep, he tripped on a stone and fell on Mi-she-kae (Turtle), who was sunning on the beach. At that time, Mishekae was not as we know her today. She had no shell and was comprised of soft skin and bone.

Turtle complained loudly to Nanaboozhoo to watch where he was going. Now, Nanaboozhoo felt ashamed of his clumsiness and apologized to Mishekae. He wondered, "What can I do to make it up to her?" He wanted to do something to help his friend. "I'll have to sit and think it over," he thought, as he followed the path back to his wigwam.

Some time later, he returned to the beach and called for Mishekae. Turtle poked her head through the soft beach mud. Nanaboozhoo picked up two large shells from the shore and placed one on top of the other. He scooped up Mishekae and put her right in the middle, between the shells.

Nanaboozhoo took a deep breath and began. "You will never be injured like that again," he said slowly. "Whenever danger threatens," he continued, "You can pull your legs and head into the shell for protection."

Nanaboozhoo sat beside his friend on the beach and told Mishekae his thoughts. "The shell itself is round like Mother Earth. It has a round hump which resembles her hills and mountains. It is divided into segments, like the many tribes that are a part of her; each different and yet connected by her."

Mishekae seemed very pleased with this and listened intently. "You have four legs, each representing the points of direction; north, south, east and west," he said. "When the legs are all drawn in, all directions are lost. Your tail will show the many lands that the Anishnabek have been and your head will point in the direction to follow."

"You will have advantages over the Anishnabek," he went on. "You will be able to live in the water as well as on land and you will be in your own house at all times."

Mishekae approved of her new self and thanked Nanaboozhoo for his wisdom. Moving now in a thick shell, she pushed herself along the shore and disappeared into the water.

So, ever since that accident long ago, Turtle has been special to the Anishnabek. To this day, she continues to grace Mother Earth, still proudly wearing those two shells.

The Snake Skin Legend

It was the time when the first animals had just been created. As Brother Snake slithered along, he felt strange and hot. He went to Nanaboozhoo and told him, "I feel uncomfortable and too warm. What can I do about it?" Now, Nanaboozhoo had many other animals telling him of their discomforts. He knew that they relied on his wisdom and advice. He pondered a long time on this and finally decided to ask the Great Spirit what to do.

He and Mukawgee went to the place where the Great Spirit usually could be found. He knew that he could get answers there. This place seemed to have a soothing effect on both of them. All of the plants and trees seemed to be perfect there; it was neither hot nor cold, but always just right.

As he related Snake's feelings to the Great Spirit, he told how many of the other animals felt the same way. Great Spirit looked at Mukawgee and asked him, "How do you feel about yourself?" Mukawgee thought about this and said, "Some days I am too hot. Then I go down to the river and cool off. When Nanaboozhoo and I are not near a river or lake, I have to wait until we get back."

The Great Spirit pondered. He thought he had made everything just right. He told Nanaboozhoo that he would have to think on it.

Some time later, he came back and said to Nanaboozhoo, "I have the solution. It seems that Snake's skin doesn't stretch with him as he grows. So, we shall let him crawl out of it when he feels strange and hot. Mukawgee's fur seems to be too much for him at times, so I shall provide him the ability to shed his hair when he gets hot. In fact, all the animals shall have a built in body part that will take care of them. Birds of the air will get lighter feathers, the deer will get thinner hair and blend into the woods. This I will do for my brothers and sisters."

Happy with this, Nanaboozhoo went back to Snake and told him to gather all the animals. Nanaboozhoo told them what the Great Spirit had related to him. They shouldn't be surprised if their hair fell out, or if they lost their skin. Thinner hair would grow on the fur animals, lighter feathers on the birds and new skins on the snakes.

When you see a discarded snake skin, think of that first snake. Were it not for him and his concern for his discomfort, it probably would have been a long time before the animals would have worked something out to adapt to Mother Earth's seasons.

The First Storyteller

Along time ago, there was an old man that the villagers called Kee-wae-zee. Every day he walked through the village on his way to his favorite place in the woods. He never talked to anyone, so the people assumed him to be a grumpy old man.

Keewaezee wasn't a grumpy old man. It was just that he stopped talking to people since his wife went on the long walk. He moved deep into the woods where he could be by himself with his thoughts. He became good friends with the animals and had long conversations with them. They exchanged views, shared food and they gave Keewaezee great companionship. So, indeed, he did have many friends.

One day while walking through the village, a little boy, dared by his friends, went up to Keewaezee and walked with him. The little boy, afraid of the "grumpy" old man, hung back. Wanting to show off for his friends that he wasn't afraid, he slowly stepped closer. Keewaezee, seeing the little boy, said, "Come with me." Hearing softness in his voice, the boy followed him and soon they were talking and laughing.

As time passed, word spread in the village that Keewaezee wasn't grumpy. They saw that he was a kind and caring man who had much to talk about. They noticed that he

11

especially liked to talk to the children. He told them things that their mothers and fathers didn't know. Before long, the children of the village looked forward to Keewaezee's coming. They knew that what he talked of came straight from his heart.

Keewaezee liked his new village friends and was soon telling them stories and legends from long ago. This he knew he was good at and it seemed to be his purpose in life.

The Tribal Council could see how wise the old man was and they invited him to live with them in the village. They gave him the choicest spot. It was on a little knoll that overlooked the wigwams and had the best berries, herbs and trees. This was their thanks to him for sharing his knowledge.

As time passed, he grew older and his body became bent. His walk was slower and he used a cane. Still, he had much to tell. Most of the children he first taught had grown up and they in turn told their children Keewaezee's stories.

One day, near winter's end, the children came to hear Keewaezee. As he shuffled outside of his wigwam, he told the children to all sit in a circle. He told them, "This is my last story. I am going on the long walk. When I am gone, let my wigwam stay. Leave my body here, because I'll be back some day." The next day, the people of the village waited for Keewaezee to come out of his wigwam. He never appeared. It was just as he said. He had gone on the long walk.

Time passed and his wigwam crumbled. Soon all plant life on the hill was gone. It was a barren place. The people looked sadly at the hill. They waited patiently for their old friend to return, but it seemed that there was no sign of him.

Then, after the first snow, when Brother Sun started getting warm and the plants and trees became green, the people saw a tall twig growing on the knoll. They watched it rise and spread out. It was the first oak tree on Mother Earth. This was Keewaezee. He had come back to them as a tall, strong oak tree.

So the people, in memory of their first storyteller, held their meetings and told stories under the tree. Keewaezee had returned as the mighty oak, giving the people the first council tree on Mother Earth.

The Song Of Wabemee

At one time there was only one kind of pigeon. Wa-be-mee (Pigeon) had a beautiful song, never heard anywhere before. He was always trying to improve it so that he could be the very best singer on the Earth Mother. As time went on, he told his mate, "I must sing even better!" It became an obsession with him and soon his competition became fired by jealousy.

He would hear the other birds sing and try to imitate them. His notes never sounded quite like theirs.

One day, when Wabemee tried to sing like the other song birds, Nanaboozhoo heard him and said, "You're trying to sound like others, but you cannot." Wabemee quickly told him, "I want to be the best singer in the bird family. I must sing better than the others." Nanaboozhoo said, "You have your own beautiful song that the Great Spirit gave to you. What more do you want?" Wabemee lost patience with Nanaboozhoo and scolded him for not agreeing that he should be the best singer. He stalked off.

Wabemee kept trying to imitate all the birds and caused some concern in their world. The other birds were content with their songs, why wasn't Wabemee happy with his?

One day at the council meeting, Song Sparrow told Nana-boozhoo about the birds' concern. He was causing confusion for their children and their mates. Nanaboozhoo decided to talk to him once more.

So, Nanaboozhoo met Wabemee one day down at the stream. He told him that his mocking was causing discord among the birds and he warned him to keep only to his own song. Wabemee was unconvinced.

As time went by, Nanaboozhoo noticed that Wabemee was mocking even more than before and he became concerned for the other birds in the village. They seemed to be more and more upset. He knew that he must go to the Great Spirit with this problem.

He went to the highest hilltop and told the Great Spirit that Wabemee was trying to be the best singer on Mother Earth. The Great Spirit said, "I know of Wabemee's jealousy, but greed shall do him in. Tell the other birds to be patient."

At the next council meeting, Nanaboozhoo told the birds what the Great Spirit had said and they waited obediently.

One day Wabemee heard another song. He wanted to master that trill also. He began to sing. One note was very high. He tried to reach it, but could not. He became very frustrated. He thought, he must sound that note and he forced himself to sing until his throat became dry and sore. Still, he forced the high note. He stopped to take a drink of water and try again, but then only low moaning sounds came out of him. From that day on Wabemee no longer had songs, just a low, soft moan.

A Garden Of Eden

Old legends say that it was a long time ago, perhaps it was when Mother Earth was just created, when all Indian people lived as one in a big village. The Great Spirit fulfilled all their needs. The lakes and rivers were teeming with fish and in the middle of the village grew a huge tree which bore all sorts of fruits and vegetables. On its limbs grew apples, pears, peaches, potatoes, beans and carrots. The people depended on the tree for their food.

As time went on, the people began to argue and grow angry with one another. One day the Great Spirit told them to change their ways and get along. They didn't listen, so the Great Spirit sent a violent storm and blew the tree over.

The people looked at the tree lying on the ground. Their existence depended on the tree and now it was gone. What would they do? They tried to exist on the fish and animals, but they went hungry. Many of them grew sick and weak.

They held a council and many things were discussed, but it all came back to the big tree. How could they get the tree back? They knew they must try to appease the Great Spirit. Perhaps they should talk to Pe-nay-wog (Many Partridge) for he was an old man who knew everything.

They went to Penaywog and told him of their plight; how the tree that furnished them with all their food was destroyed by a storm. Penaywog, knowing that the Great Spirit destroyed the tree because of their careless ways of living, told them that this was their punishment for not following what the Great Spirit had commanded. Now they must raise their own food. "How do we do that?" they asked. Penaywog said, "Go to the tree, pick up the leaves and branches, dig up the ground and put them in. You will have to tend these plants forever. This is your punishment for not doing what the Great Spirit asked."

They went back to the village, took the leaves from the tree and planted them. Some time after working in the hot sun, pulling weeds and hoeing, fruits and vegetables began to appear. They harvested the crops and remembered that they should get along with one another and live in balance with the Earth Mother.

The Rainbow Legend

When Nanaboozhoo created the flowers, they were all the same white color. Not satisfied, he and Mukawgee retired to their favorite hillside and made a mixture of colors for the flowers.

Soon he was at the task of painting all of the flowers, when two small birds began arguing. This kept up until they began to chase one another, flitting about in the trees and bushes. They swooped back and forth, close to where Nanaboozhoo was painting and he was kept busy chasing them away.

Now, he had the pots of colors all set out when the birds landed nearby. He quickly shooed them away, but when the birds tried to get out of his way, they accidentally stepped into the pots of paint. They flew up in the air, one still chasing the other and landed across a small pond. As they flew, the colors of red, blue and yellow dribbled from their feet and formed an arc of colors. With Brother Sun shining on them, the colors seemed to glow.

So today, when rain clouds gather and Brother Sun plays hide-and-seek among them, you can still see the rainbow of colors. To many of the Anishnabek, when the rainbow appears, it tells the story of Nanaboozhoo, the flowers and those two pesky birds who upset the paint pots and made the colors in the sky.

The Council Meeting
at Gitchi Wequeton

Talking with elders and remembering what my father told me, has led me to believe that the old Anishnabe villages were located about ten miles apart. They were usually found near the mouth of a river or around the headwaters coming from a lake. Some villages were seasonal, with the people moving back and forth from northern to southern Michigan. To the Anishnabek, this was a necessity for food gathering and hunting.

The elders tell a story, some 300 years past, about a council meeting which brought together Anishnabe leaders from many of their villages. They gathered to discuss their concerns about the strange men that were entering the lands of the Mohawk and Iroquois.

Chi-wee-bit (Big Tooth) decided that he must attend the council meeting. He packed his supplies, loaded up his canoe and left his village of Mich-i-ganing (Northport). As he paddled south along the deep blue waters of the bay, he saw Brother Raccoon searching for food; turning over rocks, feeling around for crayfish, and occasionally catching a small fish. He saw many deer coming to the water's edge for a cool drink.

Chiweebit paddled into a cove and before him lay the village of Omena. His brother Waboose (Rabbit) lived there, so he stopped to visit. As was the custom, he was invited to eat and stay for a time. After a good meal, the brothers talked and exchanged news of their villages. Chiweebit told his brother of his destination, Gitchi-Weque-ton (Big Bay or Traverse City), where the council meeting was to be held. They talked of the many chiefs and elders of the surrounding villages that would be gathering there. Chiweebit figured it would take him just one sun to get there, stopping at villages along the way to renew old acquaintances. As he left, he told his brother that he would stop on his return journey and tell him all the news of the meeting.

Leaving Omena, he noticed other braves of the village fishing for the Mackinaw trout, which was so plentiful. He waved as he went by, being careful not to scare the fish. Farther down the shore he came to the village of Peshawba, another place known to him as a small boy. Perhaps he should stop, but it was getting late in the day, so he continued on. He paddled near the shore under the protection of huge trees that broke the wind. The water wasn't too rough and the day was beautiful. The soft wind blew gently. Chiweebit watched animals along the lakeshore getting a drink and saw the many ducks slowly swimming by. Off in the distance the call of the loon filled the air. High overhead Brother Eagle was looking for a fish for his supper. What sweet bliss this was. He wished the day would never end.

Far ahead he saw smoke from a village. He knew from previous journeys that this would be Gitchi Wequeton. He would stay the few nights at the home of his cousin,

Maingon (Wolf). As he approached the village, the blurred outlines of wigwams began to take shape. Everyone in Gitchi Wequeton was busy with daily chores. As he beached his canoe, the children of the village came down to see the stranger. Then they rushed off, spreading the news that a visitor from Michiganing had arrived.

The council met the following day. Their concern was the news from the Mohawks and Iroquois that strange men with pale skins were coming in large boats, pushed by the winds. What did they want? What was their purpose? Were they a threat? What should the council do? All these questions had to be addressed at the meeting.

It was an important gathering and Anishnabe leaders came from as far north as Nada-way-quay-amsheing (Point Of Land In Water or St. Ignace), Gata-oda-noong (Old Village or Mackinaw City), Ahna-mie-wa-ti-going (Place Of The Holy Tree or Cross Village), Sha-boe-guning (Going Through or Cheboygan) and Be-tas-iga (Place of the Rising Sun or Petoskey). They met with great concern about the tall strange men who were exploring farther west into the big lakes region. There were reports that made the Anishnabek wonder what manner of people they were? They had hair on their faces and they wore clothes that were hard and shiny. They had strange customs so different from the Anishnabek.

The council wondered what effect these strangers would have on the people if they should ever come to their shores? A plan of action had to be prepared for the day when they might appear.

The elders discussed all sides of the issue and finally decided that the Anishnabek should be prepared. The people must first be informed, through council meetings, held in all of the villages in Anishnabe country. Then later, everyone would meet at a central location to consider all views. With this decision made, the leaders and their parties left for their villages, each one hoping that a solution could be reached. They would return to their own small villages and talk to elders in hopes that they would lend wisdom to the situation.

As Chiweebit left for home, concerns about the strangers were deep in his mind. He would spread the news of the council's decision among those villages that he passed on his return home. He knew that now it was their concern as well. Paddling his canoe, he thought of many new things; inner feelings of fear he had never experienced before. As he skimmed along the serenity of the waters, the wood's beauty and the animal brothers and sisters had a calming effect on him. By the time he reached his village, most of these feelings seemed diminished.

Beaching his canoe, he stood on the shore and looked across the water. Brother Sun was going down, a red ball on the horizon. Another day was ending and soon the night animals would be out. What could ever match what the Great Spirit put here for his people? Slowly, he went home to tell what had happened at Gitchi Wequeton. Perhaps some day in the near future, he would visit a village in the north to inform them of the council meeting. Perhaps the disturbing thoughts would some day go away.

The First Toad

When the Great Spirit was designating areas for all the creatures to live, he placed the frogs near the waters and damp regions. They were contented there. With their coloration of green and their spots, they could hide easily in the grass from their enemies.

Now, as the frogs grew and multiplied, they began to break up into small colonies. They sought out places where there was ample food and the habitat was just right.

There was a big frog who knew that he was big. He would brag and push the smaller frogs around. He always got the choicest morsels of food. He kept this up and the smaller frogs complained to Nanaboozhoo who told them that they should think of a way to get the best of this bully frog.

The big frog continued his antics and the smaller frogs began plotting how to get rid of him. It seemed that every time they would find a new place for food the big frog would come in, push everyone aside and gorge himself, leaving the smaller frogs hungry. They all agreed that he had to go. He wasn't listening to the leader any more and he was becoming mean and grumpy.

One day the small frogs had an idea. They would challenge him to a race where the food was plentiful, but also where there were many obstacles along the way.

On a bright, sunny day, they knew conditions were right and that the big frog was hungry. So, they told him of their discovery of much food, but that it was some distance away. The big frog's hunger was too much for him to resist, so he went along with the smaller frogs.

They came to the first spot and they naturally let him eat his fill. They couldn't do anything about it. He gorged himself and then they went to the next spot. On the way, they had to jump across a sandy ravine. The little frogs jumped across with ease. The big frog, bloated up with food, barely made it across. At the second place he gorged himself again. The smaller frogs, seeing that he was getting full and moving slower, told him of yet another place.

Again, they had to cross the ravine and the little frogs jumped it with ease. The big frog jumped, but didn't make it. He fell back into the ravine, rolling and tumbling to the bottom. As he rolled, the sand and small stones stuck to his skin. He tried to shake them off, but with the moistness of his skin and the heat from Brother Sun, they stuck to him.

From that day on, he looked different, with lumps and warts on his skin. So, this big greedy frog became the first toad and now lives in places where decent frogs wouldn't ever go.

Waboose and Pitchi

There was a time when only the Indian nations existed in this country. Among the Anishnabek, there were two small boys who were close friends. They watched the warriors go on their raids and hunting trips and longed for the day when they would be old enough to take up the trail of the hunter with the older men.

Each day after their schooling with the elders, Waboose (Rabbit) and Pitchi (Robin), would talk of things that they would do when they became warriors. They always tried to outdo and outtalk one another. One day while talking and telling stories, they were overheard by Chi Amick (Big Beaver). He quickly told the boys that talking like the bluejay is not telling the truth. "Remember," he said, "Bluejays holler to make everyone hear them." So, Waboose and Pitchi quieted their boasting, but not for long. Soon they could be heard again like quarreling red squirrels. This time Nanaboozhoo heard them and he came down on them like the heavy rains in the spring. He told them that to boast of such things was like crossing a swift, fast river. "You may be washed away," he said. The boys went to Mey-doo-mo-yeah (Old Woman) and asked why it was so bad to boast, because they talked of things they would do some-day. She said, "If you talk like that, then it will be expected of you." Heeding these words of wisdom, they vowed never to boast again.

After two snows, things began to look different for them. Waboose and Pitchi had grown bigger and thought surely now they could talk of things they soon would do with the older warriors. The boys were of the age when Anishnabe tradition required them to prove themselves worthy of becoming braves. Not wanting to wait for the ritual with the elders, the boys decided they would surprise the people of the village and go on their own hunt. They saw themselves returning triumphant with many skins and food for the whole village.

Plans were laid and provisions secretly gathered and hidden away. Their objective was to hunt in the large swamp where only a few braves ventured. The swamp was known to be dangerous because of its density and it was the home of Muckwa, the bear. Muckwa only wanted the seclusion of the swamp for herself and her family and this was respected by the Anishnabek. She would roar loudly scaring off anyone that ventured near. Now Waboose and Pitchi thought that this would be the place to go. They knew that the swamp would have much game and many herbs to collect.

So early one morning they packed their provisions and left for the deep swamp. Being young, they failed to realize where Brother Sun was when they went into the swamp and so they had no way of knowing their way back to the village. The swamp was thick with brush and once inside they saw game. Quickly, they set their snares and traps and began searching for herbs. As Brother Sun went down, they feasted on berries and nuts. They drank the tea of winter-

green and spent their first night in the swamp. They built a large fire to keep Muckwa away, but during the night they failed to get up and tend the fire.

Now Muckwa was mad because they had entered her swamp. She decided to roar loudly and scare them off. She crept close to where Waboose and Pitchi were sleeping. She took a deep breath and roared louder than she ever had before. The boys were so frightened that they ran in different directions. They ran so far that each found himself alone, deep in the swamp. They started calling for one another, but it was no use, they had run too far and the swamp was too dense.

The people of the village waited, but Waboose and Pitchi never returned. They were lost in the swamp forever. Still today, late at night when the screech owl calls from deep in the swamp, the people think of the two boys still searching for one another, through the many years.

The Red Headed Woodpecker

Long ago, Nanaboozhoo walked among the Indian people, listened to their problems and offered assistance to those who were hungry, sick or cold. As he was walking one day, he went to a wigwam of an old woman who lived all alone. She cared only for herself and helped no others in her village. She was busy building a fire near her wigwam. The old woman was a picture with her black fur robe, woven cap of red and apron of light buckskin. She stood by the fire and fanned the flames.

Now Nanaboozhoo, with his special powers of taking on different forms, had chosen to be a ragged, hungry old man. His hair was white as new fallen snow and his beard was long and thick. His body was bent with age and his face, wrinkled by the sun, seemed thin and weak.

When he appeared there, the old woman didn't recognize him. The old man said, "Please help me, I am hungry and have come from a long way off. I am weak and need some food. I can hardly go on." The old woman said, "Rest while I make a cake of corn." She took some of the cornmeal and put it into the fire to bake. "Migwetch," (Thank you) smiled the old man. Soon the old woman went over to the fire to look at the cake. She was surprised, the cake was so big. She thought that it would be a little one and she didn't want to give the old man such a big cake. Quickly, she put the cake away and told him that she would bake another, as that one had fallen apart. The old man appeared tired and said that he would wait.

Then the old woman took a smaller portion of cornmeal and mixed another cake. When that cake was baked, it was bigger than the first one. She said to herself, "This is such a nice cake, I'll save it for myself." She told the old man that the fire was too hot and the cake had burned up, but she would make another. The old man said that he'd wait. This time the old woman used less meal than before, but when she took that cake from the fire, it was bigger than ever!

The old woman was upset. She couldn't understand why each cake was larger than the one before. She didn't realize that it was Nanaboozhoo's magic that made each cake larger than the other. "I can't give away the nicest and biggest cake that I ever baked," she thought. She looked at the old man and said firmly, "I have no food for old beggars! Go and don't bother me any longer!"

Now, Nanaboozhoo was angry when he heard this. He rose to his feet and said, "Old woman, you should be kind and good, but you are selfish. You can't be an old woman any longer and live in your nice warm wigwam. You must go to the woods and hunt for your food in the bark of the trees!"

Nanaboozhoo raised his arms and as he did, the old woman began to get smaller and smaller. Soon she turned into a little bird. Nanaboozhoo turned her black robe into shiny black feathers and her buckskin apron changed to white feathers. The red cap became a bunch of feathers on her head. Soon, black wings came from each side of her body and she flew into the woods.

Ever since that day, she has lived in the forest. All day long she runs up and down the trees looking for food. The stiff feathers of her tail help her to sit on the tree's trunk while she pecks away with her bill, drilling holes in the trees, looking for bugs.

When you hear tapping in the woods, listen and remember the selfish old woman who wouldn't share her food with a hungry old man. Today, she is the red headed woodpecker.

The First Signs of Spring

Nanaboozhoo and Mukawgee were strolling along, looking for some brook trout. This was their favorite fish, because of the solid red meat. Now, they had come a long way from home and they were determined, looking forward to a grand meal.

They knew that the brook trout favored the cool waters of the cedar swamp in the shade of overhanging branches. As they walked, they saw the swamp getting thicker. There, just as they thought, were many brook trout. The farther they went into the swamp, the bigger the trout were. After fishing for awhile and picking out the choicest fish, they left the swamp. They were famished and decided to eat before they arrived home.

While Nanaboozhoo built a fire, Mukawgee went to the creek for some clay. The two also gathered big basswood leaves. When the fish were cleaned, they wrapped them in the leaves and packed clay around them. Then, they buried them in the hot coals.

At the edge of the swamp, they gathered black raspberries. As they picked the berries Cottontail Rabbit appeared with her little ones, playing in the berry bushes. They ran and hid among the thorny shoots, jumping and tumbling around with one another. Nanaboozhoo noticed as they ran through the bushes, that bits of their hair became tangled on the thorns. He cautioned them against losing their hair, but they paid him no attention and went on with their play.

It was some time later, when again Nanaboozhoo and Mukawgee came to this same old fishing spot. There, where the rabbits had played, a strange bush grew. Each thin branch had small hair, like tufts at the ends. These we know today as pussy willows, one of the Earth Mother's first signs of spring.

Clouding the Eyes of the Hunter

Along time ago, there was a village of Anishnabek living near what is now Charlevoix. They had their camp near the shore of the great Lake Michigan.

In this village were good hunters who were skilled in many ways. They were taught the knowledge of hunting from the Old Ones; reading signs, tracking and stalking. Now, the hunters were very wise and were sought out for their advice.

Among the hunters was a young man called Zhingons (Little Weasel). Zhingons took pride in being a good hunter and he provided much food for his village. He was looked upon with favor by all the people. The young women admired him for his abilities and said, "What a good husband he would make." This caused some problem among the other young men. They were jealous, but had to admit that Zhingons was the best hunter.

The more that Zhingons was praised, the more boastful he became. Soon, he went out hunting just to be admired. He hunted when there was no need for food. He forgot the law of the Anishnabek, to use only meat that was needed. He was breaking the natural law.

The animal brothers and sisters couldn't understand why Zhingons was hunting and killing them when there was no need. They felt unsafe in their own woods.

The animals held a council meeting and discussed their problem with Zhingons. They all agreed he had become a threat to them and that something must be done. "How can we teach him a lesson?" they wondered. They talked and talked, but to no avail. No one wanted to be near Zhingons, because they knew their life would be in danger.

The animals went to Nanaboozhoo and told him about this. He also knew that Zhingons was the best hunter, but he didn't have any ideas either. So Nanaboozhoo went to the Great Spirit. The Great Spirit answered, "You must cloud his eyes." Nanaboozhoo wondered how he could cloud Zhingons' eyes, when the clouds were always high in the sky.

The next day, he and Mukawgee were up early, preparing breakfast. The fire was going well and Nanaboozhoo needed some water to make bread. He gave Mukawgee a pail made of birch bark and told him, "Go get some water from the creek." Mukawgee, always glad to help, bounded down to the creek, got the water and came running back. As he neared the fire, he tripped and spilled the water. A cloud of steam arose from the flames. Nanaboozhoo was going to reprimand him, but he couldn't see him. There was a cloud of steam coming from the fire. Suddenly an idea came to him. When Zhingons went hunting, he would build a fire and sprinkle on small amounts of water, creating a cloud.

From that time on, the animal brothers and sisters have been protected by the fog from the eyes of the hunter. Perhaps Zhingons will always be among us.

North Wind Meets His Match

Among the many species of ducks on Mother Earth is the fish duck. Long ago, when it started to get cold on the Earth Mother, Keego-she-sheb (Fish Duck) flew south. She grew tired of having to leave her home each year. So, one particular year, she decided to stay in the north for the winter.

She began building a warm nest and when she finished, she laid in a supply of wood for a fire. She picked out four pieces of dry oak, thinking that each long log would burn approximately a month or so. This, she thought, would carry her over the cold winter months and provide enough warmth.

Now Keegoshesheb was from a strong, hearty family of ducks. When North Wind began to blow his coldest and turn the water into ice, Keegoshesheb broke the ice. Then she could search for the fish to eat under the ice. Each time she went out, she would bring extra fish home to stock up on, because an inner sense told her to lay in a supply of food. She knew that winter would stay for a long time.

One day, North Wind noticed Keegoshesheb gathering fish and decided to make it harder on her. He blew with more strength than before and made it snow even more.

Soon, big drifts were piled up around Keegoshesheb's house, but no matter, she was snug in her nest.

North Wind decided to pay Keegoshesheb a visit. He knocked on the door and blew his way in. "Come sit down, enjoy my fire," she said calmly. As they talked of the weather, Keegoshesheb mentioned how it seemed not to affect her. She had her supply of food and plenty of logs for the fire. "What's the matter," she laughed, "Your wind doesn't seem that cold, have you lost your strength?" She added some more wood to the fire and stretched out to enjoy its warmth.

Now, North Wind was getting angry. "What's the matter with this duck?" he said to himself. No other bird or animal had ever defied him before. The longer he stayed, the more Keegoshesheb tormented him with her gibes.

Soon North Wind could take no more heat, or insults, so he made his departure. Some old Anishnabek say that this is why we sometimes have an early spring. North Wind has tired and left, while Keegoshesheb is laughing.

The Eagle Who Flew Too High

Grandfather once told me, when we were out on the trap line, how the Great Spirit reacts when too many animals live on Mother Earth. Years of trapping had provided Grandfather with a special knowledge of our animal brothers and sisters. He could predict weather and seasonal climate by the size of the animal, condition of the fur and how many he harvested that year. He could also forecast the next year's animal population just by observing animal life, their behavior, and numbers.

One of nature's regulators is the scavenger buzzard. You can see him circling and soaring high overhead in search of prey, usually the dying or dead. Yet it was not his role in the old world of the Anishnabek.

There was once a family of eagles and they were the strongest of all birds that flew above Mother Earth. In this family was a young eagle who could fly higher and better than all the rest. One of his younger brothers was very jealous of him. One day the younger eagle was disturbed and angry, because again his brother flew higher and stronger in the sky. Jealousy overtook him and he began to wonder how he could come out ahead?

An idea came to him. He could challenge his older brother to a series of contests based on speed and aerobatics. His brother agreed, but one by one, the younger eagle lost every contest. There was just one event left; who could fly the highest?

They waited for a calm, clear day and then the contest began. He would let his older brother go first, then he himself would fly higher than any other eagle had ever flown. All of the other eagles gathered to watch the event. The older brother went first, up and up he flew, catching

the wind currents, and getting higher until he was just a speck in the sky. When he slowly descended, the other eagles cheered him loudly and greeted him upon his return.

The younger eagle, jealous and angry, started up on his flight. He would fly differently. He went straight up into the clear sky, determined to win. As he picked up speed, getting higher and higher, he could hardly see the other eagles below on Mother Earth. Just a little farther, he thought, and he would beat his older brother. One last big burst of speed took him higher than he had ever been before. He knew he had finally won.

Just as he was getting ready to turn back, a sudden updraft caught him and carried him higher. He tried to fly down, but he couldn't. The wind was pulling him toward the sun. He was getting hotter and still the updraft swept him up. His flight was helpless and out of control. The heat became unbearable and soon he blacked out. When he came to, he was tumbling toward Mother Earth. Nearing the crowd of eagles he could hear them laughing at him. The beautiful white feathers on his head were singed off by the heat of the sun. His head was naked.

Nanaboozhoo told him that this was a punishment for his jealousy. That from this day on, his head would be naked and he would be a scavenger of the dead animal brothers and sisters. This would be his means of existence. So from that day on, the eagle who flew too high became a buzzard and ever since then has been feeding on the carrion of the Earth Mother.

The Loon Legend

The first loons were built differently than those we know today. They were beautiful birds with colorful plumage and a lovely high call. Their feet were evenly placed in the middle of their body so that they could walk on the land and swim with ease.

Now, Mong (Loon) was a sight to see. His sleek body made him feel very proud of himself. He would stand at the water's edge and admire his beauty. He would stand before all the other water birds, telling them just how handsome he was.

The other birds became tired of his boasting. They went to Nanaboozhoo and complained. They told him how Mong acted and said that he was a nuisance. Nanaboozhoo said that he would talk with Mong.

When Nanaboozhoo saw Mong near the water the next day, he reprimanded him. He reminded Mong that all must live in harmony on Mother Earth.

Mong said that he was very sorry and that he would try. Now, as the days passed, Mong did try, but each time he looked into the water he saw his beautiful reflection. He believed that he was superior to all his brothers and sisters.

Nanaboozhoo told the water birds to be patient. He said, "One day Mong will do himself in."

The water birds decided to avoid him. They stayed away from his home on the lake so that they wouldn't have to hear his taunting. They were tired of him.

Many days later, Mong swam by the ducks and began to show off. He decided to show them how deep he could dive and get the choicest fish.

Down he dove. He noticed that the biggest fish were in the deep water. So he dove into the very deepest part of the lake.

Down and down he went, farther than he ever had before. He spotted the big fish and he swam towards them. The fish scattered and headed for the weeds. Mong followed them and the weeds became thicker. He keep on going even though it seemed harder for him to swim in the tangle of weeds. Suddenly, the weeds were so thick that he couldn't move. His feet were caught. He struggled, but to no avail.

As he strained to get loose, Mong knew that his air supply was running out. His lungs seemed about to burst. He had to get free.

In one last effort, he again lunged up. His body began to stretch and he felt his feet being pulled back. Then, he broke through the weeds and was near the surface of the water. As he sprang up, gasping for air, he swallowed some water. He coughed and struggled for air.

Mong lay in the shallow water near the edge of the lake. He shouted his call and it came out as a long, broken wail. What had happened to his beautiful call? He tried again and just as before he gave a long wail.

He looked into the water and saw his reflection. His beautiful body was gone. Now his body was long from the straining and stretching in the weeds. His feet were pulled way back near his tail feathers.

Mong tried to pull himself to the beach, but his feet were now placed so far back on his body that he could hardly walk on land.

So, the fate of Mong the loon is to forever live in the water. Today, his evening wail is for the mistake his ancestors made so long ago.

The Legend of the Cedar Tree

When the animals and plants were created on Mother Earth, each one was placed in a suitable location. The plants were asked where they wanted to live. Each one chose a spot that had good soil, wind, sun, and rain.

Most of the trees wanted to be on a hill or high ground where they would be closer to Brother Sun's warmth. They also wanted a good view.

Each tree, the maple, beech, pine, and oak chose not to live in the moist valley. This wetland had no plant life and was barren.

As the cedar tree looked for a good spot, she saw a winding stream running through the valley. This stream pleased her and she decided that she could fit in there.

She went to the Great Spirit and asked about the valley. The Great Spirit answered that her choice in the wet lands was a good one and would have its rewards. Although she didn't know what these rewards would be, the cedar tree agreed. She asked to be granted just one favor. She wanted to be able to spread thick roots just beneath the ground. That way she would be well anchored and able to drink enough moisture.

The Great Spirit thought about it and granted her wish.

So, off to the valley went the cedar tree, happy and sing-

49

ing as she went. Meanwhile, the trees on the hill were laughing. They mocked her saying, "Your feet will always be wet!" Little did they know that her roots would be different from theirs.

In a few years, other cedar trees grew next to her in the valley. She was happy, because she had company. Soon the whole valley was covered with large cedar trees. The stream ran clear and cool amongst them. Brook trout discovered the stream and the covering from the overhanging cedar roots.

Many bugs and insects also sought out the cover of the cedars. This brought the birds who loved the cedar's thick branches. Now, all the cedar trees were happy because each one had become the home of song birds. Soon, Waboose (Rabbit) discovered this wonderful place and thought it was an ideal spot for his family.

When winter came the cedar trees broke the cold wind. The snow hung on their thick green branches and became a perfect home for many animal brothers and sisters.

As the cedar trees looked up at the maples and beeches on the hill, they saw that they were naked of their leaves. The cold breath of winter chilled their branches and they stood shivering high on the hill.

The cedar trees remembered then the rewards that had been promised. Now they understood. The cedar still remains in the wet lowlands, blessed with the companionship of many animal friends.